10 Octobre 1

Bon Anniversair.

Jocelyne Clénis

Congratulations for your
Birthday.

J.K.Lee.

ranz Kafka of Prague

Jiří Gruša

Franz Kafka
of Prague

Translated from the German by
Eric Mosbacher

Schocken Books · New York

First American edition published by Schocken Books 1983
10 9 8 7 6 5 4 3 2 1   83 84 85 86
© 1983 S. Fischer Verlag
Copyright 1936, 1937 by Heinr. Mercy Sohn, Prague
Copyright © 1925, 1926, 1935, 1946, 1947, 1948, 1949, 1953,
1954, 1958, 1971 by Schocken Books Inc.
Copyright 1930, 1936, 1941, 1954, 1956 by Alfred A. Knopf Inc.
Photographs by Jiří Gruša
Published by agreement with Secker & Warburg, London

Library of Congress Catalog Card No. 83-42723

Manufactured in Great Britain
ISBN 0-8052-0748-1

The Marienschanze gun

Raban looked at the clock on a fairly high tower, which seemed to be quite close, in a street farther down the hill; just for an instant a little flag fastened up there was waved against the clock face. A swarm of little birds flew down, forming an unstable but level plane. It was past five o'clock. Raban set down his suitcase, which was covered in black cloth, leaned his umbrella against a door stone, and set his pocket-watch, a lady's watch, which he wore on a narrow black ribbon round his neck, by the clock on the tower . . .

This provincially idyllic scene from Kafka's early fragment of a novel *Wedding Preparations in the Country*, is so precisely situated in Prague that it can be identified on a map of the city. At that time, in 1907 or thereabout, Prague had not yet been transformed into that somewhere and everywhere that was to become the synthetic landscape of the mature Kafka (though to Czech eyes the original contour-line of the *genius loci* still peeps through); and it was as a reassurance that astronomically (or rather astrologically) everything was – and still is – in order, that this flag was raised day after day, pointing in the direction of Hradschin, on the gallery of the Dienstenhof observatory in the Clementinum, where watch was kept on the star of the Austro-Hungarian Empire. Raising the flag like this was the signal to fire given at midday every day by the official responsible for royal and imperial time-keeping to the royal and imperial artificer who served the gun. Clocks on towers all over the city were checked by it, officials adjusted their watches, and even the ordinary citizens of Prague, like Raban, tried somehow instinctively, at any rate for the moment, to synchronise in the old traditional way their inwardly divergent time with that of these stone towers. It was as if their sense of insecurity could be overcome by this gesture, as if there were something permanent in time in general. For clock-tower time is an institution, it is (or was) something to take refuge in, and falling in with it meant sheltering in its ancient, blessed peacefulness. But clocks in Bohemia were already diverging. In the Jewish quarter they seemed from the outside actually to be going backwards; in the palaces of the Kleinseite, for that was where the clock-face of the ancient Roman Empire pointed to, they seemed to have stopped in 1806; and there seemed to be something wrong with the Czechs if they had watches and clocks at all and the Czech souls were not still oriented in peasant fashion, so far as time was concerned, to chickens and the sun. While the German chronometer seemed to be ticking ever more hectically in its impatience to create some sort of order, to demand definite decisions, to start counting again from nought so as to be able to find out where you really were – as if nought did not offer a small but hardly ignorable opportunity to descend into the realm of negative numbers.

No, time in Bohemia had been shaken, and only the gun acted as at least a formal corrective. For the boom died away and the startled pigeons went back to their pecking among the Prague cobblestones. All forms of coexistence and cooperation and of ruling and governing, and (let us call it) relation to the supersensuous had become uncertain. Castle, ghetto and village, which had hitherto been symbols of firm anchorage, were on the move, and Prague, which as the biggest village, the biggest small town, was the remnant that held the three together, was really adrift on an iceberg. This tectonic shift had long been in preparation. When post-Reformation Bohemia was reconstructed by force from above, a unity in the form of baroque culture was imposed on it. This overrode the particularism in religion and politics that had previously prevailed, but it was based on the principle of separate roles for castle and village (with the ghetto beehive stuck on). In contrast to other countries, not only a social but also a more or less ethnic stratification was involved here, at any rate in those fields in which the three constituent elements found their clearest expression. For all the bloodshed that accompanied its origin, this community was ultimately fruitful and left a lasting mark on those involved. Superficially it was patched together with Habsburg yarn, though with its mandarin-like officialdom, its nobility, its lack of independence, its army that was primarily an imperial and only secondarily a Bohemian army, this was actually done by that 'Confucian' institution – the Austrian Empire. This almost 'Chinese' state religion (there was nothing exotic about Kafka's use of metaphor) could survive only so long as its baroque foundation survived, or so long as it was capable of being transcended through and in the latter.

In the course of nearly a century of struggle with the Enlightenment, which (like Kafka's nomads) came from the north, it demonstrated an incredible durability, but eventually it succumbed. The attempt by the state somehow or other to revive the past got bogged down in bourgeois philistinism, in romantic rationalism, the luxuriant efflorescence of which spanned the age in which a different kind of unity based on – let

us call it – elective affinity, might perhaps have been attainable. The birth of an individual named Herrmann Kafka coincided with the beginning of the movement from below that resulted in the separation into its component parts of what in times past had been joined from above. Almost instinctively the castle retired increasingly into itself. As it had presided over the surroundings in a manner that was more step-fatherly than fatherly, there was no difficulty in regarding it as alien and devoid of *auctoritas* (devoid of authority, but also bearing in mind the derivation from *augere*, seeing and being seen, being open with oneself); for the obviousness of its purpose was questioned without its ceasing to be the seat of full living and the will to be. That merely emphasised the distinct nature of the castle and its secrets, though it nevertheless remained alluring, like Room 13, the prohibition to enter which only increases the temptation to break in – in case there is anything inside. Thus the nineteenth century in Bohemia was the century of the conquest of the castle, and – with Kafka – also that of the attempt to force one's way into it. The village paradoxically became depopulated, for it grew bigger. This took place to the extent that it was a typical Czech community, purposefully reduced to its underground essence, its Slavonic nature and the latter's more matriarchal character (which in any case made the Bohemian village incomprehensible to the patriarchal castle). It was determined to gain possession of this structure on the top of the hill, but the way up to it led away from familiar territory, meant solid ground vanishing from beneath one's feet, and – again paradoxically – getting used to a fuller life and imposing one's will from this point of view implied *willing* in agreement with all the willing that had been done in the past, i.e., seigniorial willing. But for this the interruption had been too long, and no appeal to the *status* quo ante succeeded in completely bridging over the feeling of helplessness, the deep-seated habituation to living at a lower level – beneath the castle. Thus in a way the path to a history of their own began with a childish acceptance by the Czechs of having no history. Also these conquerors of the castle were dangerously stigmatised by their plebeian behaviour.

The ghetto opened up too, and in a way that was just as deceptive, as if it were in the middle of a chasm that had developed between the village and the castle. The tendency was to decline rather than the reverse, and those who worked their way out of it suddenly realised that they carried their origin with them.

Time ticked away at three different rates. Three communities were vitally affected by loss of identity. That was the *Trial* that took place there. Austria, that 'humanity in miniature', was its world laboratory. That was something that the Marienschanze gun could no longer cover up. Instead it emphasised the provincial equipment of the laboratory, which contrasted so significantly with the experiment that was being conducted in it. The back-cloth against which it took place was a small-town back-cloth because, for all their sullen aloofness from one another, village and castle, and of course ghetto too, were reduced to a dreadful, simple-minded petty provincial level in which the grotesque flourished. For it too was simple-minded and dreadful.

For the time being the three remained together. From the centre of it all, from the centre of Bohemia and the very centre of the city, there emerged Franz Kafka. They were still planning the future, which they felt to be something working for them in the rhythm of time, their own time. Only in the chasm – in which the former ghetto stood – and (most probably) from it was it possible to see that the future could also be something that came crashing down on human beings; that time could also be the end of time and

the present failure and questioning – a dreadful *Metamorphosis*. Raban-Kafka's eyes were perceptive enough to see that. In contrast to the eyes of the castle folk, they shared with the village the experience of the pariah, but they were not plebeian eyes, for in them there shone the consciousness of an ancient and chosen origin; and also of course a hereditary sense of the last days, as well as of a *Judgment* over them. Hence Kafka could 'abolish time' without his 'today and yesterday' passing away. Later he was to write:

He has two antagonists: the first pushes him from behind, from his birth. The second blocks the road in front of him. He struggles with both. Actually the first supports him in his struggle with the second, for the first wants to push him forward; and in the same way the second supports him in his struggle with the first; for the second is of course trying to force him back. But it is only theoretically so. For it is not only the two protagonists who are there, but he himself as well, and who really knows his intentions? However that may be, he has a dream that some time in an unguarded moment – it would require too, one must admit, a night darker than any night has ever been yet – he will spring out of the firing line and be promoted, on account of his experience of such warfare, as judge over his struggling antagonists.

Jiří Gruša

The unapproachable castle – a typical feature of the country. Kafka's *Castle* should not be associated with a definite place, for every locality of any size in Bohemia was dominated by a castle which was unapproachable by the unprivileged who lived all round it. Dealings with the castle were conducted exclusively through intermediaries. The always slightly condescending fashion in which orders were passed down was based on a sense of superiority resulting partly from the elevated position, but chiefly on the belief that those down below, whether Germans, Czechs or Jews – each category was regarded with greater contempt – were mere commoners and servants.

But the castle of castles was that which dominated Prague and, according to the point of the compass card that pointed towards Vienna, belonged to Count South. Generally he was not there, and it was occupied by all sorts of senior and junior officials. Steep steps led up to it from the town, past houses with crumbling plaster and peeling paint – resembling the many streets 'down below' in 'the town', where the humble and compliant, characterised by their 'staunch cooperative spirit' lived, people with 'positively tortured faces' and 'swollen lips'.

I see a town in the distance. Is that the one you mean? It is possible, yet I do not understand how it is possible you can make out a town there, I can only see something there since you have drawn my attention to it, and, even so, no more than some vague outlines in the mist. Oh yes, I see it all right, it is a mountain with a castle on the top and houses, like those of a village, on the slopes. Then it is that town, you are right, it is actually a large village.

In Czech Prague – *Praha* – is feminine, like
the words for night, love and death. It lies
beneath its castle, but unlike it was never
unapproachable or closed, but on the
contrary, receptive of everything and all-
embracing, as if determined to swallow or
get the better of it, thus at the same time
remaining true to itself. This 'mother'
equipped with claws fascinated all who
came under her sway. For a thousand years
she produced crossbreeds, thoroughbreds
and half-breeds, weak and strong, Germans,
Czechs and Jews, who in the 'fifth quarter'
down below sang: 'A thousand ages in Thy
sight are but an evening gone.'

*Now it is remarkable and I am continually
surprised by the way we in our town humbly
submit to all orders issued in the capital. For
centuries no political change has been brought
about by the citizens themselves. In the capital
great rulers have superseded each other – indeed
even dynasties have been deposed or annihilated,
and new ones have started ... Our officials have
always remained at their posts; the highest
officials came from the capital, the less high
from other towns, and the lowest from among
ourselves – that is how it has always been and it
has suited us.*

The town and the 'fifth quarter'. Though the
ghetto was officially abolished in 1852, it
preserved its appearance, its peculiarities
and its atmosphere until the turn of the
century.

In Hebrew my name is Amschel, like my mother's maternal grandfather.

Kavka František, *obch. s uhlím. VII. Veverkova ul. 721.
— Frant., obuvník. II. Petrská ul. 12.
Kafka Frant., povozník. Sm. Švarcenberkova tř. 13.
— Frant., sluha v čekárnách spol. rak. uh. st. dr. Žk. Veleslavínova ul. 18.
— Frant., úč. oficiál fin. zem. řed. Vnhr. Slezská tř. 2.
Kavka Frt., veř. posluha. II. Spálená ul. 48.
Kafka František, vetešník. I. Perlová ul. 7.
Kafková Frant., vdova po ber. inspektoru a maj. domu. Koš. Plzeňská tř. 101.
— Hedvika, obch. s mýdlem, svíčkami a voňavkami. Krl. Palackého tř. 41.
Herrmann Kafka, obch. se zbožím ozdobným, modním, trikotovým, slunečníky, deštníky, holemi a bavlnou, přís. soudní znalec (telef. 141). I. Celetná ul. 3.
Kavková Hermina, industr. učitelka. II. Hopfenštokova ul. 8.

21*

Franz Kafka officially bore his father's Czech name, that derives from the word *kavka*, jackdaw. According to Bohemian country lore, this small member of the crow family possesses the gift of soothsaying. Prague, city of a hundred towers, has always kept them within its walls, in spite of the belief that a town over which a swarm of these creatures suddenly appeared was exposed to the evil spirit of war.

At the beginning of the century several persons of that name were living in Prague. Herrmann Kafka, Franz's father, who had arrived there from southern Bohemia in far from prosperous circumstances and worked himself up the hard way 'with very little money', was the only one of them whose name was distinguished in the town directory by an anchor, indicating that he was a certified consultant to the commercial court. He had, as it were, cast anchor underneath the castle.

The directory entry read as follows:

> Herrmann Kafka, linen, fashionable knitted ware, sunshades and umbrellas, walking sticks and cotton goods, sworn consultant to Commercial Court I, (telephone 141), Zeltnergasse 3.

I should have been happy to have you as a friend, as a chief, an uncle, a grandfather, even indeed (though this rather more hesitantly), as a father-in-law. Only as what you are, a father, you have been too strong for me . . . a true Kafka in strength, health, appetite, loudness of voice, eloquence, self-satisfaction, worldly dominance, endurance, presence of mind, knowledge of human nature, a certain way of doing things on a grand scale, of course also with all the defects and weaknesses that go with these advantages and into which your temperament and sometimes your hot temper drive you. You are perhaps not wholly a Kafka in your general outlook . . . You had worked your way up so far alone, by your own energies, and as a result had unbounded confidence in your own opinion . . . From your armchair you ruled the world. Your opinion was correct, every other was mad, meschugge, *not normal. With all this your self-confidence was so great that you had no need to be consistent at all and yet never ceased to be in the right. It did sometimes happen that you had no opinion whatsoever about a matter and as a result all opinions that were at all possible with respect to the matter were necessarily wrong, without exception . . . For me you took on the enigmatic quality that all tyrants have whose rights are based on their person and not on reason. At least so it seemed to me.*

You have a particularly beautiful, very rare way of quietly, confidently, approvingly, smiling, a way of smiling that can make the person for whom it is meant entirely happy. I can't recall its ever having expressly been my lot in my childhood, but I dare say it may have happened, for why should you have refused it to me at the time when I still seemed blameless to you and was your great hope? For the rest, such friendly impressions in the long run brought about nothing but an increase in my sense of guilt, making the world still more incomprehensible to me.

This house, No. 1/21, corner of Maiselgasse and Karpfengasse, known as the 'tower house', was not a very good address. Visitors who came here from the Kleiner Ring by way of the Laubengang in the direction of the 'fifth', the Jewish quarter, could not fail to notice the pungent smell of *Schnapps* that emerged from the disreputable Batalion bar half-hidden in a low basement.

It was to this house that Herrmann Kafka brought his bride. She was 'unquestionably the right woman for him'; she came of a 'good' Jewish family named Löwy that had long been established at Podebrad. In the year 5643 after the Creation she bore him a son.

The building known as the 'green frog house' opposite is the only one at the edge of the 'fifth', or Jewish quarter that survived the 'clean-up' of the neighbourhood that began in 1893.

Left: The 'tower house' in 1983.
Above: The view from the door of that house of what was then known as the 'chicken market' before the demolition of the old houses.

'Half cat, half lamb' – the son, in whom his father hoped to take pleasure, dressed to look as if such a thing might really have been possible. The photographer, conscious of his station and slightly over-impressed, discerned the 'cross' between lamb and cat and detected what Franz's father was only beginning to suspect; namely, that the 'good-class Jewish family' from Podebrad was much too soft for what he had in mind for the boy.

It is a legacy from my father, half cat, half lamb. But it only developed in my time; formerly it was far more lamb than cat. Now it is both in about equal parts. From the cat it takes its head and claws, from the lamb its size and shape; from both its eyes, which are mild and changing.

A fine wound is all I brought into the world; that was my sole endowment.

Josefstadt was the name adopted by the
ghetto as a mark of gratitude to Emperor
Josef II, who behind this synagogue on the
Rote Ring ordered the iron gate that
separated the 'fifth quarter' from the rest of
the city to be left open for ever. But it was
not so easy to pass through it, for doing so
did not mean automatically leaving the 'fifth
quarter' behind.

*The Altneu synagogue yesterday. Kol Nidre.
Suppressed murmur of the stock market. In the
entry, boxes with the inscription: 'Merciful gift
secretly left assuage the wrath of the bereft.'
Churchly inside. The pious, apparently eastern
Jews. In socks. Bowed over their prayer books,
their prayer shawls drawn over their heads,
become as small as they possibly can.*

Joseph K. came from this fully utilised space beneath the castle', where the Jews lived like a colony of bees whose queen was regularly taken away; from a town that possessed the comforting sense of community of a village; it had now obviously been opened, but it withdrew into itself all the more for that reason. It was a world of its own in which law no longer seemed to apply, swarming with half-naked children, where women went about their personal affairs before the eyes of their neighbours. Midday and evening meals were eaten out of doors, and on summer evenings, when the heat indoors was stifling, scurrilous exchanges took place between door and door and window and window in Czech, German and Yiddish in a jargon intelligible to few outsiders. The devout who observed the holy days lived next door to brothels, and drunks bawled from taverns while the murmur of prayers came from synagogues close at hand.

In my memory I could still clearly see the room next to the kitchen, where sometimes, though seldom enough, we were able to huddle together, while next door in the kitchen the rest of the family were carrying on their quarrels, of which there was never any lack. It was a small dark room with an ineradicable smell of coffee in it, for the door to the kitchen, which was even darker, was open day and night.

Narrow lanes led off the Milklasgasse. Shops and stalls at which everything from old shoes to rusty old iron was on sale often only concealed the principal trade, prostitution.

(p. 30) The Jewish town hall, in which in 1912 Kafka made a short speech introducing the actor Jizchak Loewy at a Yiddish recitation evening; (p. 31) the Zigeunergasse. It was at the synagogue here that in July 1896 Kafka was called on for the first time to read from the Torah.

I have three sisters, one married, one engaged; the single one, without prejudice to my affection for the others, is easily my favourite.

Ottla, born 1892, the member of the trio who was unmarried in 1912, was Kafka's favourite – a 'lamb' who was not really a lamb, but a cat with claws; Elli (Gabriele), born 1889, the one who was married in 1912, was most like Kafka and reminded him of himself; she was violent, morose and full of guilt, and broke away from the circle marked by the anchor of the certified court consultant Herrmann Kafka, her domineering father; Valli (Valerie), born 1890, who in 1912 was the engaged member of the trio, was the prettiest and was the closest to being a Löwy 'lamb'; she was not only pretty like her mother but like her had a very definite mind of her own.

The window looking into the 'cathedral' in the flat in the 'house of the Three Kings', No. 3 Zeltnergasse, where Kafka prepared for his barmitzvah to the accompaniment of organ music and a choir. The window enabled him to see right into the cathedral, the Teyn church. The aisle on the right from where he stood is stated formerly to have contained the mortal remains of a twelve-year-old Jewish boy named Simon Abeles who was killed by his father in 1693 after admitting that he had been converted to Catholicism. This is now recalled by an inconspicuous memorial tablet. Six days later, according to the legend, when the secretly buried body was exhumed, it is stated to have been 'of natural colouring, completely unrigid, and pleasing to look upon'. What is certain is that the boy's father hanged himself with his prayer-thong in his cell in the town hall in the Old City. Nevertheless he was then executed in baroque fashion; the body was dragged to the town gate, where 'the heart was taken from the body and stuffed into the Jew's mouth for this pitilessness to his own flesh and blood.'

'My father is still a giant of a man,' said George to himself.
'It's unbearably dark here,' he said aloud.
'Yes, it's dark enough,' answered his father.
'And you've shut the window too?'
'I prefer it like that.'

Some say the word Odradek is of Slavonic origi‌
and try to account for it on that basis. Others
again believe it to be of German origin, only
influenced by Slavonic.

Staircases, lofts, entrance halls, corridors.
Also children playing in foreign languages
who responded abruptly or actually
aggressively if they were addressed wrongly.
Children's games with pathetic toys that
they made themselves out of paper, string
and twine, e.g. a *špulka* that could be made
out of a cotton reel.

At first glance it looks like a flat star-shaped
spool for cotton, and indeed it does seem to have
thread wound upon it: to be sure, only old,
broken-off bits of thread are eligible, not merely
knotted but tangled together, of the most varied
sorts and colours. But it is not only a spool, for
a small wooden cross-bar sticks out of the
middle of the star, and another small rod is
joined to that at a right angle. By means of this
latter rod on one side and one of the points of the
star on the other, the whole thing can stand
upright as if on two legs . . .
'Well, what's your name?' you ask him.
'Odradek,' he says. 'And where do you live?' 'N‌
fixed abode,' he says, and laughs.

The confined spaces of the Old City led to *Angst*, the fear of being shut in, claustrophobia. Kafka went this way daily to the elementary school in the Fleischmarktgasse. The smell from the shops spread all the way to the Jakobskirche and penetrated to the school rooms. In the evening these lanes and alleys were the haunt of the most squalid prostitutes, who were called *holátka, fuchtle, flundry* . . . and also *kavky* (jackdaws).

The row of houses was often interrupted by brothels . . . the last room of all the houses was again a brothel . . . The wall across from the door . . . therefore the last wall of the row of houses was either of glass or merely broken through . . . To the left was a solid wall, on the other hand the wall on the right was not finished, you could see down into the court, even if not to the bottom of it, and a ramshackle grey staircase led down in several flights.

Kavky (jackdaws) from the Ungelt, a quiet old courtyard, about 1900. Such women may have stood here at the corner of the Langegasse and the Fischergasse for two hundred years. At the Zum Deyl inn right behind Kafka's elementary school they sang:

> Deyl all night keeps watch and ward.
> Protector of the *kavky* horde.

Their heads looked as if they had been beaten flat on top and their features as if the pain of the beating had twisted them to the present shape.

In 1893 men with pickaxes began the so-called clean-up of the Old City. In the course of the next twenty-two years building after building was demolished in order to adapt that part of the city to the requirements of hygiene.

Those residents who like Herrmann Kafka had done relatively well in the world had long since given up their homes there so as to be able to shake off the humiliations and memories of the ghetto.

At first all the arrangements for building the Tower of Babel were characterised by fairly good order, indeed the order was perhaps too perfect ... In fact the general opinion at that time was that one simply could not build too slowly ... People argued in this way: The essential thing in the whole business is the idea of building a tower that would reach to heaven. In comparison with that idea everything else is secondary. The idea, once seized in its magnitude, can never vanish again; so long as there are men on the earth there will also be th irresistible desire to complete the building ... S why exert oneself to the extreme limits of one's present powers? There would be some sense in doing that only if it were likely that the tower could be completed in one generation. But that is beyond all hope. It is far more likely that the next generation with their perfected knowledge will find the work of their predecessors bad, and tear down what has been built so as to begin anew. Such thoughts paralysed people's power ..

All the legends and songs that come to birds in that city are filled with longing for a prophesied day when the city would be destroyed by five successive blows from a gigantic fist. It is for that reason too that the city has a closed fist on its coat of arms.

I was stirred immeasurably more deeply by Judaism in the Pinkas synagogue.

At the time of the 'clean-up', with the ghetto being demolished all round them, the synagogue became the symbol of traditional piety. The older generations now prayed in temples, but to the younger generation these seemed empty.

I found equally little means of escape from you in Judaism. Here some escape would, in principle, have been thinkable, but more than that, it would have been thinkable that we might have found each other in Judaism or even that we might have begun from there in harmony. But what sort of Judaism was it I got from you?

Every day Julie Kafka fetched her son from the 'German-language state grammar school in Prague' and brought him home to the 'burrow'. Meanwhile – 'Jewish grammar-school boys are easily recognised with us' – the friends Hugo Bergmann, Emil Utitz, Paul Kisch, Oskar Pollak and Felix Weltsch, and in addition to these Max Brod, who went to another school, discussed the future of the world. After their school-leaving examination they all left the city, while Kafka relapsed for ever into that place of executions and public celebrations.

I have changed my place, I have left the upper world and am in my burrow, and I feel its effec at once. It is a new world, endowing me with new powers, and what I felt as fatigue up there is no longer that here.

An entrance can deceive, can lead astray, can give the attacker no end of worry, and the present one can do that at a pinch. But a really serious attack has to be met by all the reserves in the burrow and all the force of my body and soul – that, of course, is self-evident. So the entrance can very well remain where it is.

Kafka after taking his school-leaving examination, looking out; it was a 'distracted' sort of looking out, for all the ways out of this city were merely passages somewhere else in it. The light at the end of a passage merely marked the beginning of another. Longing for the outside world but circumscribed by the Altstädter Ring, he went from Ungelt to Ungelt. Greedy for experience and knowledge, in his search for 'nourishment' Kafka was fed on fodder that had already been chewed by a thousand mouths, the sawdust of the law that he studied for his father's sake. The way to that feeding-place and back was no longer than that from school to the meat market and back. Here too there were tunnels, and the feeling of being compressed that is the fate of 'every guilty innocent being punished'.

I stride along and my tempo is the tempo of all my side of the street, of the whole street, of the whole quarter. Mine is the responsibility, and rightly so, for all the raps on doors or on the flat of a table, for all toasts drunk, for lovers in their beds, in the scaffolding of new buildings, pressed to each other against the house walls in dark alleys, or on the divans of a brothel.

The luminosity and precision of the sacred
and profane baroque buildings of Prague
influenced Kafka's writing. Max Dvořak's
discovery, in Kafka's time, of the roots of
mannerism in the baroque revealed the
closeness of that age to the present. The
kinship was pointed out to Kafka by his
friend Oskar Pollak.

*There was a time when I went every day into a
church ...*

He studied whatever he felt like, and since he did not want to be a lawyer he chose the career of an official, which seemed to suit him quite well, as the working hours are short and he has the afternoon to himself. I have known for many years that he spend his leisure hours writing. But I assumed thi to be a mere pastime . . . I would therefore very much like to ask you if you could somehow draw his attention to this fact, question him about the way he lives, what he eats, how many meals he has, and abou his daily routine in general . . . Julie Kafka.

So the only thing left for me to do would be to change myself in time, before the world could intervene, just sufficiently to lessen the little woman's rancour, not to wean her from it altogether, which is unthinkable.

Wherever the Kafka family lived this clock went with them.

On the right is the entrance to the royal and imperial regional court used by counsel and their aides as well as by judges and executioners in plain clothes. Here, in the Zeltnergasse, where Herrmann Kafka's anchor testifies to his good character. The entry against K.'s name also testifies to 'there being nothing against him'.

Someone must have traduced Joseph K., for without having done anything wrong he was arrested one fine morning.

I have a job, so a New Year has begun, and my worries, granted that until now they went on foot, now follow suit and go on their hands.

Incapable of writing for a whole year, from 1906 to 1907, surrounded by the files of th higher district court on the edge of Charles Square.

I am utterly on the downward path and – I car see far enough for that – I can't help going to the dogs.

K. liked to get away from the confinement of
office buildings and bourgeois housing. It
took him no more than half-an-hour to
make the round of the houses where his
friends lived. The faces he saw on the way
were unfriendly, but there was always his
advocate, he had only to step out of the
court building in the Zeltergasse into the
fruit market to see the Schalengasse, where
Max Brod lived, who spent a lifetime
defending every sentence that Kafka wrote.

*I ought to be in a place where all kinds of people
meet, from various parts of the country, from
every class, every profession, of all ages; I ought
to have an opportunity of choosing carefully out
of a crowd those who are kind, those who are
able, and those who have an eye for me. Perhaps
the most suitable place for this would be a huge
fair-ground.*

There were also friends from the outside
world in Prague at the time. Franz Werfel
said of them: 'Quiet things flung themselves
into my arms, quiet things that in an hour of
fulfilment I stroked like well-behaved pets.'
K., who was helpless and uncertain even in
relation to such things, sat with them in the
Café Arco at the corner of the Hybernergasse
and the Pflastergasse and admired them.

*Today in the coffee house with Werfel. How he
looked from the distance, seated at the coffee-
house table. Stooped, half reclining even in the
wooden chair, the beautiful profile of his face
pressed against his chest, his face almost
wheezing in its fullness (not really fat); entirely
indifferent to the surroundings, impudent and
without flaw. His dangling glasses by contrast
make it easier to trace the delicate outline of his
face.*

I have now examined my desk more closely and I have seen that nothing good can be done on it. There is so much lying about, it forms a disorder without proportion and without that compatibility of disordered things which otherwise makes every disorder bearable. Let disorder prevail on the green baize as it will, the same is true of the orchestras of old theatres ... Individual, relatively huge things in the orchestra appear in the greatest possible activity, as though it were possible for the merchant to audit his books in the theatre, the carpenter to hammer, the officer to brandish his sabre, the cleric to speak to the heart, the scholar to the reason, the politician to the sense of citizenship, the lovers not to restrain themselves, etc ... The next higher open pigeon hole, already hemmed in by the small closed drawers, is nothing but a lumber-room, as though the first balcony of the auditorium, really the most visible part of the theatre, were reserved for the most vulgar people, for old men about-town in whom the dirt gradually moved from the inside to the outside ... In the pigeon-hole lie old papers that I should long ago have thrown away if I had a waste paper basket ...

The Assicurazioni Generali building, October 1907 to July 1908. 'A cage went in search of a bird.' K. had hoped for other towns, for distant lands, for windows with a different view, but his cage always found him in this 'damned town'.

No, I don't get too worked up about the office; the obvious justification for my irritation is that it has survived five years of office life, of which the first in a private insurance company from eight a.m. to seven, to eight, and eight-thirty p.m. was particularly awful. There was a certain place in a narrow passage leading to my office where almost every morning I used to be overcome with such despair that a stronger, more consistent character than mine might have committed suicide quite cheerfully.

Kafka entered this building, which housed
the Austrian government Workmen's
Compensation Department, on 30 July 1908
and left it only to die. A cage had found its
jackdaw for good and all.

*He could have resigned himself to a prison. To
end as a prisoner – that could be a life's
ambition. But it was a barred cage that he was
in. Calmly and insolently, as if at home, the di
of the world streamed out and in through the
bars, the prisoner was really free, he could take
part in everything, nothing that went on outsid
escaped him, he could simply have left the cage
the bars were yards apart, he was not even a
prisoner.*

Kafka's daily itinerary took him down the
Hybernergasse past the Café Arco. Max
Brod used to wait for him 'at the Powder
Tower at two p.m. . . . Franz was always
later than I, he had something extra to do at
the office or got lost in conversation with his
colleagues.'

He ate no meat, nothing that smelled of blood. K. was physically weak, 'more lamb than cat', and he would eat only food that did not involve the destruction of others. He, whose father came of a line of kosher village butchers, was always haunted by the 'image of a pork butcher's broad knife . . . that chops into me'.

My paternal grandfather was a butcher in a village near Strakonitz. I must not eat as much meat as he slaughtered.

Perhaps the knife of the butcher would be a release for this animal; but as it is a legacy I must deny it that. So it must wait until the breath voluntarily leaves its body, even though it sometimes gazes at me with a look of human understanding, challenging me to do the thing of which both of us are thinking.

Whoever leads a solitary life and yet now and
then wants to attach himself to someone,
according to changes in the time of day, the
weather, the state of his business and the like,
and suddenly wishes to see any arm at all to
which he might cling – he will not be able to
manage for long without a window looking on
to the street.

Kafka met Felice Bauer at Max Brod's home in Prague on 13 August 1912. The meeting led to a long-distance love affair of unusual closeness. They twice became engaged and twice were obliged to recognise the futility of it. He wrote her a countless number of words – letters and stories 'for F . . .' or F.B. such as Frieda Brandenfeld (the fiancée in 'The Judgment') and Fräulein Bürstner (the fiancée in *The Trial*). With Felice Kafka never enjoyed 'the sweetness of a relationship to a woman one loves'. In one night at the beginning of their affair, that of 22–23 September 1912 he wrote the story 'The Judgment' that was the 'breakthrough' to his literary self-discovery. But his father threatened, 'Just take your bride on your arm and try getting in my way. I'll sweep her from your very side.' After the final breach Kafka suffered a haemorrhage of the lungs on the night of 9–10 August 1917.

I do not believe that the battle for any woman in any fairy-tale has been fought harder and more desperately than the battle for you within myself – from the beginning, over and over again, and perhaps for ever.

'I was just too unhappy to get up,' K. complained to Felice Bauer in November 1912 because he had been waiting in vain for a letter from her. While he was thus lying miserably in bed 'a little story' occurred to him. This was *Metamorphosis*, which reflects his personal feelings in relation to his family as well as the still-incomprehensible changes in the city, brought about by time.

In a letter
As if that weren't enough, I collided with a butcher's boy's tray outside the front door, and can still feel the wood above my left eye.

In a story
... and when a butcher's boy met them and passed them on the stairs coming up proudly with a tray on his head ...

The Graben. Prague was not only a 'damned' or gloomy city, oppressed by its own history; it also radiated a sense of being a city of the elect, with a certain propensity to regard itself as the hub of the universe. It presented a singular mixture of provinciality and quality, with a remarkable passion for literature and literary men who were determined to write masterpieces and spent their whole lives sitting at café tables talking about them. It was also a city of real masterpieces. Until the thirties the social axis of Prague was the Korso. Beneath the windows of the house in which Milena Jesenská was born it led into the so-called Golden Cross: the Ferdinandstrasse, the Obstgasse, the Graben with Wenceslas Square on the right, but was divided into Czech and German parts. The Graben was the street of fashion and luxury. It was German, German Jewish, which was why things sometimes became dramatic there. It was here that the mob gathered whenever there was a wave of unrest in nationally divided Prague, and afterwards glaziers had to replace the smashed windows. But then elegant ladies and gentlemen started appearing again late on Sunday mornings in the Café Continental (which was a shade less literary than the Café Arco), at the banks, the fashion houses and the jewellers and greeted one another in a complicated ritual of graduated bows. And the world seemed to be in order again in old Prague . and we would play

'Blocking the Road', we fixed a certain distance on the path, which one had to defend and one had to pass. The attacker was blindfold, but the defender had no means of preventing him from passing except that in the instant of passing over he touched the attacker on the arm; if he did it earlier or later he had lost. Anyone who has never played this game will think the attack is made very difficult and the defence very easy, but the fact is the very opposite, or at any rate is more frequent to find people good at attacking

View of Wenceslas Square from the Museum (all the way to the Letna). In the background the Golden Cross, the Assicurazioni Generali building on the right.

After the clean-up of old Prague it was
turned into a bourgeois city on the Paris
model. Herrmann Kafka and K. went up in
the world too. Their address was 36
Niklasstrasse, now Pariserstrasse, facing the
end of the bridge. The house has been
demolished, but the view remains.

*Early in the day already, and several times
since, I have enjoyed the sight from my window
of the triangular piece cut out of the stone
railing of the staircase that leads down on the
right from the Czech Bridge to the quay level.
Very steep, as though it were giving only a
hasty suggestion. And now, over there across
the river, I see a stepladder on the slope that
leads down to the water. It has always been
there, but is revealed only in the autumn and
winter by the removal of the swimming school
in front of it, and it lies there in the dark grass
under the brown trees in the play of perspective.*

*Without forebears, without marriage, without
heirs, with a fierce longing for forebears,
marriage and heirs. They all of them stretch out
their hands to me: forebears, marriage and
heirs, but too far away for me.*
*There is an artificial, miserable substitute for
everything, for forebears, marriage and heirs.
Feverishly you contrive these substitutes, and if
the fever has not already destroyed you, the
hopelessness of the substitute will.*

K. and Felice Bauer ended their first
engagement at the Ascanischer Hof pensic
in Berlin on 12 July 1914 in the presence
Grete Bloch, Ernst Weiss and Felice's sister
Erna.

The tribunal in the hotel. The trip in the cab.
F.'s face. She patted her hair with her hand,
wiped her nose, yawned. Suddenly she gathere
herself together, and said very studied, hostile
things she had long been saving up. The trip
back with Miss Bl. The room in the hotel; the
heat reflected from the wall across the street.
Afternoon sun, in addition.

*This being Sunday morning, most of the
windows were occupied, men in shirt-sleeves
were leaning there smoking or holding small
children cautiously and tenderly on the window
ledges. Other windows were piled high with
bedding, above which the dishevelled head of a
woman would appear for a moment. People
were shouting to one another across the street;
one shout just above K.'s head caused great
laughter. Down the whole length of the street at
regular intervals, below the level of the
pavement, there were little general grocery
shops, to which short flights of steps led down.
Women were thronging into and out of these
shops or gossiping on the steps outside. A fruit
hawker who was crying his wares to the people
in the windows above, progressing almost as
inattentively as K. himself, almost knocked K.
down with his push-cart. A phonograph which
had seen long service in a better quarter of the
town began stridently to murder a tune.*

'No,' said the priest, 'it is not necessary to accept everything as true, one must only accept it as necessary.' 'A melancholy conclusion,' said K. 'It turns lying into a universal principle.'

They paced up and down for a while in silence, K. walking close beside the priest, ignorant of his whereabouts. The lamp in his hand had long since gone out. The silver image of some saint glimmered into sight immediately before him by the sheen of its own silver, and was immediately lost in the darkness again.

The wall on the Laurenziberg – K.'s Great Wall of China – has always been full of holes. To the present day it is still called the hunger wall, having been built in the fourteenth century to give work to the hungry. Perhaps it might have been able to offer protection against enemies from all points of the compass.

Many years ago I sat one day, in a sad enough mood, on the slopes of the Laurenziberg. I went over the wishes that I wanted to realise in life. I found that the most important or the most delightful was the wish to attain a view of life (and – this was necessarily bound up with it – to convince others of it in writing), in which life, while still retaining its full-bodied rise and fall, would simultaneously be recognised no less clearly as a nothing, a dream, a dim hovering. A beautiful wish, perhaps, if I had wished it rightly.

Black flags flying in the Ferdinandstrasse
show that the Emperor Franz Josef is dead.
But mourning remains official – not long
afterwards the street was renamed National
Street and adorned with the Czech tricolour.

*Thus, then, do our people deal with departed
emperors, but the living ruler they confuse
among the dead. If once, only once in a man's
lifetime, an impartial official on his tour of the
provinces should arrive by chance at our village
make certain announcements in the name of the
government, scrutinise the tax lists, examine
the schoolchildren, enquire of the priest
regarding our doings and affairs, and then,
before he steps into his litter, should sum up his
impressions in verbose admonitions – then a
smile flits over every face, each man throws a
stolen glance at his neighbour, and bends over
his children so as not to be observed by the
official. Why, they think to themselves, he's
speaking of a dead man as if he were alive, this
Emperor of his died long ago, the good official is
having his joke with us, but we will behave as
we did not notice it, so as not to offend him. So
eager are our people to obliterate the present.*

Kafka was faced with the choice between a
'Castle' or a 'work' address, between living
in the Alchimistengasse or the Schönborn
palace – the Totengasse, the 'street of the
dead' lay in between. He chose the Castle, in
the quarter of the nobility, who talked
French and gave orders in German. His first
haemorrhage followed his admission to the
Castle.

I got up, stimulated as one is by anything new
... also somewhat alarmed of course ... walke
about the room, sat down on the bed – all the
time blood.

Away from here, simply away from here! You need not tell me where you are taking me. Where is your hand, ah I grope for it in vain in the dark. If I only had got hold of your hand, I think then you wouldn't spurn me. Do you hear me?

For the first time the 'damned town' let him go. He was off the leash, but the trial had already begun. He believed that God had sent him this illness, because without it he would never have got away from Prague.

He went to stay with Ottla, 'who had escaped into farming', who had had the courage to escape. She defied her family by buying a plot of land at Zürau (its Czech name means orphanage) and took her brother there. K. lived among these 'citizens of the earth' for a year and at first felt happy in their sympathetic proximity.

'I can't go away,' replied K. 'I came here to stay. I'll stay here.' And giving utterance to a self-contradiction which he made no effort to explain, he added as if to himself: 'What could have enticed me to this desolate country except the wish to stay here?'

*Feeding the goats; field tunnelled by mice,
digging potatoes ('How the wind blows up our
arses'); picking hips; the peasant F. (seven girls,
one of them short, a sweet look, a white rabbit
on her shoulder; a picture in the room,
'Emperor Franz Josef in the Capuchin Tomb';
the peasant K. a powerful man; loftily recited
the whole history of his farm, yet friendly and
kind). General impression given one by the
peasants: noblemen who have escaped into
agriculture, where they have arranged their
work so noisily and humbly that it fits perfectly
into everything and they are protected against
all insecurity and worry until their blissful
death. True dwellers on the earth.*

The decisively characteristic thing about this world is its transience. In this sense centuries have no advantage over the present moment. Thus the continuity of transience cannot give any consolation; the fact that new life blossoms among the ruins proves not so much the tenacity of life as that of death.

The church at Zürau as it is today.

The surprising similarity of Bohemian castles. Not only do they radiate unapproachability, they actually dominate through it. This castle at Friedland was especially important to K. He knew it from his travels on official business, and Ottla had studied agriculture here, so as to be able not only to survey the land at Zürau but also to cultivate it. At that time the castle at Friedland belonged to the Count von Clam (Klamm?) – *klam* is the Czech word for deception.

The castle in Friedland. The different ways there are to view it: from the plain, from a bridge, from the park ... from the woods through tall firs. The castle astonishes one by the way it is built one part above the other; long after one has entered the yard it still presents no uniform appearance, for the dark ivy, the dark grey walls ... enhance the heterogeneity of its aspect. The castle is really built not on a plateau but around the rather steep sides of a hill-top.

'Just listen to me, sir. Herr Klamm is a gentleman from the Castle, and that in itself, without considering Klamm's position there at all, means that he is of very high rank. But what are you? ... You are not from the Castle, you are not from the village, you aren't anything. Or rather, unfortunately you are something, a stranger, a man who isn't wanted and is in everybody's way.'

In November 1919 at the Pension Stüdl at Schelesen, north of Prague, K. wrote a letter to his father in which he tried to summarise all the reasons why he was afraid of him – but he did not post it. He remembered his 'constant mode of referring to an assistant with T.B. lungs: "The sooner he dies the better, the mangy dog." '

Sometimes I imagine the map of the world spread out flat and you stretched out diagonally across it. And what I feel then is that only those territories come into question for my life that either are not covered by you or are within your reach. And, in keeping with the conception that I have of your magnitude, these are not many and not very comforting territories.

Milena, whom he loved. M for mother, who
gives her love without conditions or
qualifications. Franz Werfel spoke of
Prague's 'threefold soul'; Milena represented
the Slavonic, feminine part of it – for in
Czech Prague is feminine. So Kafka, like
many Prague Germans and Jews, was
attracted and sought to strike root here. He,
who at first had seen only man's negative
metamorphosis into vermin, became
suddenly aware of another possible pair of
opposites, the animal and the beautiful.
Beauty and the Beast. But then he again
saw the knife of self-laceration.

*I, an animal of the forest, was at that time
barely in the forest, lay somewhere in a dirty
ditch (dirty only as a result of my being there,
of course). Then I saw you outside in the open
the most wonderful thing I'd ever seen. I forgot
everything entirely, forgot myself, got up, came
closer – though fearful in this new yet familiar
freedom – came closer nevertheless, reached
you, you were so good I cowered down beside
you as though it were my right, laid my face in
your hand, I was so happy, so proud, so free, so
powerful, so at home – over and over again this:
So at home. So at home – but fundamentally I
was still only the animal, belonged still only in
the forest, lived here in the open only by your
grace, read without realising it (for after all I'd
forgotten everything) my fate in your eyes. This
could not last.*

*Love is to me that you are the knife which I turn
within myself.*

*'I always wanted you to admire my fasting,'
said the fasting showman. 'We do admire it,'
said the overseer affably. 'But you shouldn't
admire it,' said the fasting showman. 'Well,
then, we don't admire it,' said the overseer, 'but
why shouldn't we?' 'Because I have to fast, I
can't do anything else,' said the fasting
showman. 'What a fellow you are,' said the
overseer, 'and why can't you do anything else?'
'Because,' said the fasting showman, lifting his
head a little and speaking with his lips pursed,
as if for a kiss, right into the overseer's ear, so
that no syllable might be lost, 'because I
couldn't find any food I liked. If I had found any,
believe me, I should have made no bones about it
and stuffed myself like you or anyone else.'*

The last photograph of Franz Kafka

*You raven, I said, you old bird of ill-omen, what
are you always doing on my path?*

*For the eventuality that in the near future I
may die or become wholly unfit to live . . . let me
say that I myself have torn myself to shreds.*

The reason why posterity's judgment of individuals is juster than that of contemporaries lies in their being dead. One develops in one's style only after death, only when one is alone. Death is to the individual like Saturday evening to the chimney sweep; it washes the dirt from his body.

1883

3 July: Franz Kafka born in Prague, the eldest child of Herrmann Kafka, trader, and his wife Julie, *née* Löwy

1893–1901

Attends German Grammar School in the Old City

1901–1906

Student of law at Prague University (doctorate, 1906); beginning of friendship with Max Brod

1906–1907

Practises law at the higher district court and the criminal court

1907–1908

Employed by Assicurazioni Generali insurance company

1908

Enters Workmen's Compensation Department of the Kingdom of Bohemia in Prague

1910

Begins to keep diaries

1910–1912

Trips abroad with Max Brod; contacts with Jewish theatrical company from Poland playing in Prague

1912

Meets Felice Bauer, from Berlin; his first book *Meditation* published; writes *The Judgment* and *Metamorphosis*; works on 'Lost and Not Traced'.

1913

Lively correspondence with Felice

1914

First engagement to Felice; works on *The Trial* and *In the Penal Settlement*

1915

Carl Sternheim, winner of the Fontane prize, hands over prize money to Kafka 'as a sign of recognition'

1916

Love affair with Felice resumed: 'Our contract is in short to marry shortly after the war'

1916–1917

Writes many short pieces (in particular most

of the 'Country Doctor' stories) in the
Arbeitsdomizil in the Alchimistengasse
1917
Moves to his own flat in the
Schönbornpalais; begins learning Hebrew;
falls ill with tuberculosis of the lungs and
second engagement broken off
1917–1918
Sick-leave in the Bohemian village of Zürau,
many 'Aphorisms' written
1919
Affair with Julie Wohryzek; 'Letter to his
Father'
1920
Sick-leave in Merano; beginning of
correspondence with Milena Jesenská
1921
Sick-leave at Matliary (High Tatras);
friendship with Robert Klopstock
1922
The Castle and 'Hunger Artist' written;
retirement from Workmen's Compensation
Department; writes 'Investigations of a Dog'
1923
Affair with Dora Dimant; moves to Berlin;
completes 'The Burrow'
1924
Tuberculosis of the larynx
Writes 'Josephine the Singer'
3 June: dies at Kierling bei Klosterneuburg
11 June: burial in Jewish cemetery at
Prague-Straschnitz

Key to quotations from Kafka's works edited by Max Brod

9 *Raban looked at the clock . . . Wedding Preparations in the Country*, trs. Ernst Kaiser and Eithne Wilkins (London: Secker & Warburg, 1973) (Notes), p. 432; *Dearest Father: Stories and Other Writings* (New York: Schocken Books, 1954) (Notes), p. 397

11 *He has two antagonists . . .* 'He', in *Description of a Struggle*, trs. Willa and Edwin Muir (London: Secker & Warburg, 1960), p. 298; 'He', in *The Great Wall of China*, trs. Willa and Edwin Muir (New York: Schocken Books, 1946), p. 246

14 *I see a town in the distance . . .* 'Fragments from Note-books and Loose Pages', in *Wedding Preparations in the Country* (London), *op. cit.*, p. 328; 'Fragments from Notebooks and Loose Pages', in *Dearest Father* (New York), *op. cit.*, p. 299

16 *Now it is remarkable . . .* 'The Refusal', in *Description of a Struggle*, trs. Tania and James Stern (London), *op. cit.*, p. 89; 'The Refusal', in *Description of a Struggle*, trs. Tania and James Stern (New York: Schocken Books, 1958), p. 182

18 *In Hebrew my name is . . . The Diaries of Franz Kafka 1910–1913*, trs. Joseph Kresh (London: Secker & Warburg, 1948) (New York: Schocken Books, 1948), p. 197

20 *I should have been happy . . .* 'Letter to his Father', in *Wedding Preparations in the Country* (London) *op. cit.*, pp. 159, 164; 'Letter to his Father', in *Dearest Father* (New York), *op. cit.*, pp. 140, 145

20 *You have a particularly beautiful . . .* (London), *Ibid.*, p. 175; (New York), *Ibid.*, p. 155

24 *It is a legacy from my father . . .* 'A Crossbreed', in *Description of a Struggle* (London), *op. cit.*, p. 113; 'A Crossbreed', in *The Great Wall of China* (New York), *op. cit.*, p. 238

24 *A fine wound . . .* 'A Country Doctor', in

In the Penal Settlement, trs. Willa and Edwin Muir (London: Secker & Warburg, 1973), p. 138; 'A Country Doctor', trs. Willa and Edwin Muir in *The Penal Colony* (New York: Schocken Books, 1961), p. 142

26 *The Altneu synagogue ... The Diaries of Franz Kafka 1910–1913*, *op. cit.*, p. 72

28 *In my memory ...* 'Fragments from Note-books and Loose Pages', in *Wedding Preparations in the Country* (London), *op. cit.*, p. 390; 'Fragments from Notebooks and Loose Pages', in *Dearest Father* (New York), *op. cit.*, p. 355

32 *I have three sisters ... Letters to Felice*, trs. James Stern and Elisabeth Duckworth (London: Secker & Warburg, 1974) (New York: Schocken Books, 1973), p. 22

34 *My father is still a giant ...* 'The Judgement', in *In the Penal Settlement* (London), *op. cit.*, p. 50; 'The Judgment', in *The Penal Colony* (New York), *op. cit.*, p. 54

36 *Some say the word Odradek ...* 'Troubles of a Householder', in *In the Penal Settlement* (London), *op. cit.*, p. 156; 'The Cares of a Family Man', in *The Penal Colony* (New York), *op. cit.*, p. 160

36 *At first glance it looks like a flat star-shaped spool ...* (London), *Ibid.*, pp. 156–157; (New York), *Ibid.*, pp. 160–61

39 *The row of houses was often interrupted by brothels ... The Diaries of Franz Kafka 1910–1913*, *op. cit.*, p. 89

41 *Their heads looked as if they had been beaten flat ... The Castle*, trs. Willa and Edwin Muir (London: Secker & Warburg, 1953), p. 35; (New York: Schocken Books, 1974), p. 29

42 *At first all the arrangements for building the Tower of Babel ...* 'The City Coat of Arms', in *Description of a Struggle* (London), *op. cit.*, p. 99; 'The City Coat

of Arms', in *The Great Wall of China* (New York), *op. cit.*, pp. 245–46

42 *All the legends and songs that came to birth in that city ...* (London), *Ibid.*, p. 100; (New York), *Ibid.*, p. 247

44 *I was stirred ... The Diaries of Franz Kafka 1910–1913*, *op. cit.*, p. 72

44 *I found equally little means of escape ...* 'Letter to His Father', in *Wedding Preparations in the Country* (London), *op. cit.*, p. 191; 'Letter to His Father', in *Dearest Father* (New York), *op. cit.*, p. 171

46 *I have changed my place ...* 'The Burrow', in *Description of a Struggle* (London), *op. cit.*, p. 197; 'The Burrow', in *The Great Wall of China* (New York), *op. cit.*, p. 111

46 *An entrance can deceive ...* (London), *Ibid.*, p. 185; (New York), *Ibid.*, p. 93

48 *I stride along and my tempo is the tempo of all my side of the street ...* 'The Way Home', in *In the Penal Settlement* (London), *op. cit.*, p. 31; 'The Way Home', in *The Penal Colony* (New York), *op. cit.*, p. 34

50 *There was a time ...* 'Conversations with the Suppliant', in *In the Penal Settlement* (London), *op. cit.*, p. 3; 'Conversations with the Suppliant', in *The Penal Colony* (New York), *op. cit.*, p. 9

52 *He studied whatever he felt like ...* Letter of Julie Kafka in *Letters to Felice*, *op. cit.*, p. 46

52 *So the only thing left for me to do ...* 'A Little Woman', in *In the Penal Settlement* (London), *op. cit.*, p. 232; 'A Little Woman', in *The Penal Colony* (New York), *op. cit.*, p. 238

54 *Someone must have traduced Joseph K ... The Trial*, trs. Willa and Edwin Muir (London: Secker & Warburg, 1956), p. 7; *The Trial*, trs. Willa and Edwin Muir (New York: Schocken Books, 1968), p. 1

56 *I have a job ... Franz Kafka, A Biography*

by Max Brod (New York: Schocken Books, 1960), p. 73

56 *I am utterly on the downward path* . . . *Franz Kafka, A Biography* by Max Brod (New York: Schocken Books, 1960), p. 69

58 *I ought to be in a place* . . . 'Advocates', in *Description of a Struggle* (London), *op. cit.*, p. 142; 'Advocates', in *The Complete Stories* (New York: Schocken Books, 1971), p. 450

60 *Quiet things* . . . 'Ich habe eine gute Tat getan', *Das Lyrische Werk* by Franz Werfel (Frankfurt: 1967), p. 60

60 *Today in the coffee house with Werfel* . . . *The Diaries of Franz Kafka 1914–1923* (London: Secker & Warburg, 1949) (New York: Schocken Books, 1949), p. 31

62 *I have now examined my desk more closely* . . . *The Diaries of Franz Kafka 1910–1913*, *op. cit.*, pp. 37–38

64 *A cage went in search of a bird* . . . 'Sin, Suffering, Hope . . .', in *Wedding Preparations in the Country* (London), *op. cit.*, p. 40; 'Reflections on Sin, Pain, Hope', in *The Great Wall of China* (New York), *op. cit.*, p. 281

64 *No, I don't get too worked up about the office* . . . *Letters to Felice*, *op. cit.*, p. 48

66 *He could have resigned himself to a prison* . . . 'He' in *Description of a Struggle* (London), *op. cit.*, p. 291; 'He' in *The Great Wall of China* (New York), *op. cit.*, p. 267

68 *At the Powder Tower at two p.m.* . . . *Franz Kafka, A Biography*, *op. cit.*, p. 62

70 *'Image of a pork butcher's broad knife'* . . . *The Diaries of Franz Kafka 1910–1913*, *op. cit.*, p. 286

70 *My paternal grandfather was a butcher* . . . *Letters to Milena*, trs. Tania and James Stern (London: Secker & Warburg, 1953) (New York: Schocken Books, 1953), follows p. 75, line 16 (previously unpublished)

70 *Perhaps the knife of the butcher* . . . 'A Crossbreed', in *Description of a Struggle* (London), *op. cit.*, p. 115; 'A Crossbreed', in *The Great Wall of China* (New York), *op. cit.*, p. 241

72 *Whoever leads a solitary life* . . . 'The Street Window', in *In the Penal Settlement* (London), *op. cit.*, p. 36; 'The Street Window', in *The Penal Colony* (New York), *op. cit.*, p. 39

74 *I do not believe that the battle for any woman* . . . *Letters to Felice*, *op. cit.*, p. 525

76 *I was just too unhappy to get up* . . . Ibid., p. 47

76 *As if that weren't enough, I collided with a butcher's boy's tray* . . . Ibid., p. 11

76 *. . . and when a butcher's boy* . . . 'Metamorphosis' (here called 'The Transformation') in *In the Penal Settlement* (London), *op. cit.*, p. 126; 'The Metamorphosis', in *The Complete Stories* (New York), *op. cit.*, p. 138

80 *'Blocking the road'* . . . 'Fragments from Note-books and Loose Papers', in *Wedding Preparations in the Country* (London), *op. cit.*, p. 245; 'Fragments from Notebooks and Loose papers', in *Dearest Father* (New York), *op. cit.*, p. 223

82 *Early in the day already and several times since* . . . *The Diaries of Franz Kafka 1910–1913*, *op. cit.*, p. 121

84 *Without forebears* . . . *The Diaries of Franz Kafka 1914–1923*, *op. cit.*, p. 207

86 *The tribunal in the hotel. The trip in the cab* . . . ibid., p. 63

88 *This being Sunday morning, most of the windows were occupied* . . . *The Trial* (London), *op. cit.*, p. 43; *The Trial* (New York), *op. cit.*, p. 34

92 *'No,' said the priest* . . . (London), Ibid., p. 246; (New York), Ibid., p. 220

95 *Many years ago I sat one day* . . . 'He', in *Description of a Struggle* (London), *op. cit.*, p. 292; 'He', in *The Great Wall of China* (New York), *op. cit.*, p. 267

96 *Thus, then, do our people deal with departed emperors* ... 'The Great Wall of China', in *Description of a Struggle* (London), *op. cit.*, pp. 85ff; 'The Great Wall of China', in *The Great Wall of China* (New York), *op. cit.*, pp. 168ff

98 *I got up, stimulated as one is by anything new* ... *Letters to Milena*, *op. cit.*, p. 21

00 *Away from here, simply away from here* ... 'Fragments from Note-books and Loose Papers', in *Wedding Preparations in the Country* (London), *op. cit.*, p. 265; 'Fragments from Notebooks and Loose Papers', in *Dearest Father* (New York), *op. cit.*, p. 242

02 *'I can't go away,' replied K* ... *The Castle* (London), *op. cit.*, p. 172; *The Castle* (New York), *op. cit.*, p. 180

04 *Feeding the goats: field tunnelled by mice* ... *The Diaries of Franz Kafka 1914–1923*, *op. cit.*, p. 188

06 *The decisively characteristic thing about this world* ... 'The Eight Octavo Note-books', in *Wedding Preparations in the Country* (London), *op. cit.*, p. 109; 'The Eight Octavo Notebooks', in *Dearest Father* (New York), *op. cit.*, p. 95

08 *The castle in Friedland* ... *The Diaries of Franz Kafka 1914–1923*, *op. cit.*, p. 239

08 *'Just listen to me, sir. ...'* *The Castle* (London), *op. cit.*, p. 67; *The Castle* (New York), *op. cit.*, p. 63

110 *'constant mode of referring to an assistant'* ... 'Letter to His Father', in *Wedding Preparations in the Country* (London), *op. cit.*, p. 181; 'Letter to His Father', in *Dearest Father* (New York), *op. cit.*, p. 161

110 *Sometimes I imagine the map of the world* ... (London), *Ibid.*, pp. 211–12; (New York), *Ibid.*, p. 191

112 *I, an animal of the forest* ... *Letters to Milena*, *op. cit.*, p. 199

112 *Love is to me that you are the knife* ... *Ibid.*, p. 200

114 *'I always wanted you to admire my fasting'*, ... 'A Hunger Artist', in *In the Penal Settlement* (London), *op. cit.*, p. 249; 'A Hunger Artist', in *The Penal Colony* (New York), *op. cit.*, p. 255

116 *You raven, I said* ... 'The Eight Octavo Note-books', in *Wedding Preparations in the Country* (London), *op. cit.*, p. 126; 'The Eight Octavo Notebooks', in *Dearest Father* (New York), *op. cit.*, p. 109

116 *For the eventuality that in the near future I may die* ... (London), *Ibid.*, p. 125; (New York), *Ibid.*, p. 109

118 *The reason why posterity's judgment of individuals* ... 'He', (Notes from the Year 1920) in *Description of a Struggle* (London), *op. cit.*, p. 297; 'He', in *The Great Wall of China* (New York), *op. cit.*, p. 273

NEUESTER PLAN von PRAG.

Sehenswürdigkeiten: Tramway: